The Sixteenth Chester Book of M

Christmas
& Advent Motets
for 6 voices

Edited by Anthony G. Petti

For Gerald Gifford and the Choir of Wolfson College, Cambridge

LIST OF MOTETS

CHESTER MUSIC

2

1. AD TE, DOMINE, LEVAVI

To you, Lord, I have lifted up my soul. My God, in you I have placed my trust: let me not be put to shame, neither let my enemies gloat over me. Indeed, none of those who hold fast to you shall ever be brought to confusion. (*Ps.25, i–iii*)

Andrzej (Andreas) Hakenberger (c.1574-1627)

CH55439

*Tenor and Bass 1 switched from 13 iv to the end.

2. RORATE CAELI

Pour out dew from above, you heavens, and let the clouds rain down the Just One. Let the earth open and bring forth a Saviour. (*Isaiah* 45, viii)

Jacob Handl(1550-91)

10

3. DOMINE, DOMINUS NOSTER

O Lord, our Lord, how wonderful your name is throughout the whole earth. Your greatness is praised above the heavens: from the lips of children and infants you have perfected praise because of your enemies, to silence the hostile and the vengeful. When I consider the heavens, - the moon and stars - fashioned by your fingers, I wonder what man is that you should care for him, or his children that you should look after them. You have made him little less than the angels, crowned him with glory and honour, and set him to preside over your handiwork. You have placed all things under him: all the sheep and oxen, and the cattle of the fields, the birds of the air, and all aquatic creatures that move through the pathways of the sea. O Lord, our Lord, how wonderful your name is throughout the whole earth. (*Ps.8*)

Orlandus Lassus(1532-94)

12

14

4. VENI DOMINE

Come, Lord, and do not delay. Visit us with your peace so that we can rejoice in your presence with hearts made pure. Come, Lord, and as a mother consoles her children, so shall you comfort us. We shall see you and our hearts will rejoice.

Cristóbal de Morales (c. 1500-53)

5. PASTORES LOQUEBANTUR

The shepherds said to one another: "Let us go straight to Bethlehem and see this thing which has happened,
which the Lord caused and has made known to us". So they quickly went and found Mary and Joseph, with the baby
lying in the manger. Alleluia. (*Luke 2, xv–xvi*)

Francisco Guerrero (1528 – 1599)

The Word was made flesh and lived among us, and we saw his glory, a glory befitting the Father's only Son, full of grace and truth. (*John 1, xiv*)

Hans Leo Hassler(1562-1612)

7. GLORIA IN EXCELSIS

Glory to God on high and peace on earth to men of good will. The host of angels rejoices because eternal salvation for the human race has appeared. (First sentence, *Luke* 2, xiv)

Giovanni Maria Nanino (c. 1543-1607)

34

8. O MAGNUM MYSTERIUM

How great a mystery and how wonderful a sacrament, that beasts should see the new-born Lord lying in their manger. We have seen the baby and the chorus of angels praising the Lord. Alleluia.

Giovanni Pierluigi da Palestrina(c. 1525-94)

40

EDITOR'S NOTES

The aim of this series is to make more readily available a comprehensive body of Latin motets from the 16th and early 17th centuries. It encompasses a wide selection of texts from the liturgical year for the benefit of church choirs and those concert choirs that wish to present their programmes according to theme or season. In general, the motets are within the scope of the moderately able choir, though, obviously, the later volumes require fuller vocal resources than the first eight.

The editor has endeavoured to preserve a balance between a critical and performing edition. Where necessary, the motets are transposed into the most practical performing keys, are barred regularly, fully underlaid, and provided with breathing marks. They also contain a keyboard reduction, either as a rehearsal aid or as an accompaniment, since some of the later works clearly envisaged a *continuo*. Editorial tempi and dynamics are supplied only in the reduction, leaving choirmasters free to supply their own according to their interpretation, size of choir and the acoustics. The vocal range is given with the preliminaries for each motet, together with a translation of the Latin text, while a table of use is provided in the notes.

For the benefit of musicologists, the motets are transcribed from the most authoritative sources available, and the original clefs, signatures and note values are shown at the beginning and wherever they change in the course of a piece. Ligatures are indicated by slurs, editorial accidentals are placed above the stave, and the underlay is italicized when expanding a ditto sign, or enclosed in square brackets if entirely editorial. Where the original contains a *basso continuo*, it appears as the bass line of the reduction; but figurings are not included, because they are extremely sparse and do not normally indicate more than the harmony already provided by the vocal parts. Finally, each volume contains editorial notes on the scope of the selection, the composers, the motets, and the sources, together with a list of any editorial emendations and alterations.

This volume contains four six-part motets for Advent and four for Christmas. Five of them are virtually SSAATB and three are SSATBB, so that in no case is the tenor line split. Such combinations reflect quite closely the original voice distributions, and the only switching of parts that had to be made is recorded in a footnote on page 3.

The first composer, Andrzej Hakenberger, is a Polish (Pomeranian) composer, details of whose life and works are given in Volume 15. Like the motet in that volume, Hakenberger's *Ad te Domine levavi* was published in *Harmonia sacra,* 1617 (transcribed here from the copies in the British Library), and it was also included in the Peplin tablature. It is less baroque in concept than his *Exsultate justi* (Volume 15), and opens with a fugue somewhat in the Roman style of fifty years earlier, though the movement in tenths is unusual (e.g., bar 3). The word-painting is restrained, but includes, as might be expected, a gradual ascent to the end of "levavi animam meam" and *tutti* homophony for "etenim universi". The general movement of the motet is very fluid. The harmonies (which include a liberal amount of consecutive thirds and tenths) are tonal rather than modal, despite the apparent Dorian opening, the main alternation being (in this transposition) between E major and minor, with occasional incursions into the key of B. This ambivalence gives the motet an appropriately muted Advent joy, which is never permitted to overflow into exuberance, not even at the end, where the Phrygian cadence leaves a sense of expectation rather than fulfilment.

It is hard to overlook the work of Jacob Handl (1550-91) in an anthology of Latin motets, and this series proves no exception, since he features in five of its volumes (biographical details in Volume 12). This Slovene composer has remarkably refined sensibilities. He combines variety with economy, and is always keenly attuned to the nuances of the words, without recourse to madrigalian devices. *Rorate caeli* was published in his *Tomus primus operis musici,* 1586, as item no. 10 (transcribed from British Library copy). It deserves to rank alongside the more famous five-part setting by Palestrina (published separately by this editor for Chester), with which it has a few affinities, though, unlike the Palestrina, it sets the text only as far as "Salvatorem". Anyone familiar with Handl's monosyllabic *Ecce Quomodo* (Volume 4) will not fail to notice the contrast to this motet with its profusion of pleasing melismas for the key words and syllables, all providing a sense of abundance and fruition, the most bountiful phrases being reserved for "Salvatorem". Handl also shows his mastery of antiphony, alternating three upper with three lower voices for "aperiatur" before the *tutti* of "et germinet", then progressing to groups of four voices, gradually martialling all forces for the final "Salvatorem". Again, as with the Hakenberger, the mood is somewhat muted for the Advent motet by use of the Aeolian mode, though steadily moving towards the related major key in all the later cadential points.

The praise that can be lavished on Handl has to be redoubled for Orlandus Lassus (1532-94), whose mastery in every form of vocal music both sacred and secular beggars belief, and whose output is so great that it could have occupied several lifetimes of many another Renaissance composer. The biography of Lassus has been severely revised in recent years (see, for example, the article in the *New Grove*), thereby losing most of its romantic flavour. In particular, it is disappointing that the story of his being thrice abducted as a choirboy and smuggled abroad because of his beautiful voice has now to be consigned to the attic of apocrypha, and with it the supposed trauma which could have been the delight of psycho-musicologists. However, it is certain that he was born at Mons, travelled widely in his youth in the service of Fernando Gonzaga, a general of the Emperor Charles V, and that he continued his peregrinations in Italy under several other patrons. In 1563 he obtained the important post of *maestro di cappella* at St. John Lateran, but soon left to fulfil his *wanderlust.* He joined the court of Albrecht V in Munich, and became *Kapellmeister* in 1563, holding the post until his death, despite frequent absences.

Lassus' *Domine Dominus noster* was published as item 430 of his vast posthumous collection of sacred music, *opus musicum,* 1604 (transcribed here from the British Library copy), but it dates from the fifteen seventies or eighties, when, as if reverting to his short *missae breves*, he adopted a chordal, syllabic declamatory mode of writing, with short note values and hardly any repetition of text, a style sometimes termed *villanella*. Unlike the short masses, however, the motet convincingly preserves the verbal accent, and the synocapation generally emphasizes rather than disrupts the textual pointing. Harmonic interest is provided by constant variation of cadences, while light and shade in texture are greatly enhanced by the skilful deployment of different vocal combinations, though the *tutti* passages are abundant too, being invoked at all the appropriate places ("magnificentia tua", "omnia subiecisti" and "universa terra"). The monosyllabic treatment enables Lassus to set the whole of the psalm within a relatively short compass, and he provides a pleasing circularity by using the identical phrases for the beginning and the end of this vital motet. It should be noted that at least two distinct styles of interpretation are possible: in one, treating the work as truly declamatory, the speed can be varied according to the text and *rallentandi* can be used at major cadences; in the other (which is favoured by the editor), strict tempi are to be employed in a chant style such as might be expected from, say, a performance of Stravinsky's *Ave Maria*.

The fourth Advent motet is by the Spanish master Cristóbal de Morales (c.1500-53), details of whose life and works are given in volumes 3 and 14. His *Veni Domine* was first published in an anthology entitled *Il primo libro de motetti a sei voce da diversi eccellentissimi musici composti*, Venice, 1549 (complete set of copies in the Bayerische Staatsbibliothek, Munich). It is a movingly wistful motet, basically in the Aeolian mode but constantly shifting into related modes, making the application of *musica ficta* especially difficult. One of its characteristic features, much favoured by Morales, is the use of an *ostinato* part, in this case, the first alto line, which repeats not only the same text but also the same musical phrase (loosely based on the Maundy Thursday plainsong melody), each time on a lower step of the scale, so that by the fourth repetition it has descended from B to E. The texture is light and airy, with full use of vocal resources being reserved for the last few bars. There is a profusion of shapely descending phrases reinforced by poignant harmonies, most notably in the six-three passage for "ita consolaberis" (bars 35-6)–a technique often used later by Palestrina (cf. *Canite tuba*, bars 38-40, Volume 12).

The first composer in the Christmas section is another Spaniard, Francisco Guerrero (1528-99), who for a brief time was a pupil of Morales. Guerrero was born in Seville and studied music under his brother Pedro. From 1546 to 1548 he was *maestro de capilla* at Jaén cathedral, then two years after became a singer at Seville cathedral. For a short period he was *maestro de capilla* at Malaga cathedral in succession to Morales, but then took over as director at Seville cathedral. He stayed in Seville for the rest of his life, apart from visits to Rome and the Holy Land. Guerrero's sacred music is quite extensive and includes masses, magnificats, passions, a volume of villancicos, and four books of motets. He is often praised for the gentle lyricism of his music, especially when setting Marian texts, but anyone who has listened to his villancicos will recall that he is capable of writing dramatically exciting music, as in, for example, *Oyd oyd una cosa* and *A un niño llorando* (published by Chester in Guerrero, *Three Spanish carols*). The present work, *Pastores loquebantur* is also lively and varied, with appropriate changes of mood to suit the text. It begins with a bustling fugue, the hubbub of excitement among the shepherds being indicated by quick melismas, especially for the stressed syllable of "loquebantur". The speed of "venerunt festinantes" (bar 42ff.) is emphasized by monosyllabic quavers and heightened by off-beat entries in the style of the villancicos mentioned above. The pace slows considerably for "invenerunt Mariam", while for "et infantem positum in praesepio" there is a gentle, almost rocking, passage of homophony tenderly introduced by the four upper voices. The motet concludes with joyful scale melismas for "alleluia", somewhat in the style of Palestrina, similarities to which are also to be found in the opening (compare with the first few bars of Palestrina's five-part *Rorate caeli*). It should also be noted that Guerrero has given some masculine weight to the narrative of the shepherds by using two bass lines. *Pastores loquebantur* was first published in a collection of Victoria's motets, *Motecta festorum totius anni*, 1585 (near-perfect set in Christ Church College, Oxford). Four years later it appeared with a second part in Guerrero's *Mottecta... quae partim quaternis, partim quinis, alia senis, alia octonis concinuntur vocibus*, Venice, 1589 (set of copies in Colegio y Capilla del Corpus Christi, Valencia).

The larger scale works of Hans Leo Hassler (biographical details in Volume 11) often reveal Venetian influence, as might be expected from a pupil of Andrea Gabrieli. This is true to some extent of his *Verbum caro factum est*, first published in *Cantiones sacrae de festis praecipuis totius anni 4, 5, 6, 7, 8, et plurium vocum*, Augsburg, 1591 (transcribed here from the second and corrected edition, Nuremberg 1597, three copies of which are housed in the British Library). However, the style is somewhat chastened and simplified, as is appropriate for such a devotional and meditative text — at least until the "gloriam unigeniti" section, where the familiar Venetian technique of breaking into quavers coupled with short rests suddenly appears. Until that point, too, the treatment is homophonic in conventional antiphonal style, the upper voices alternating with lower voices in echo, followed by a *tutti* to close a section. The solemnity of the text is preserved by a close adherence to the Aeolian mode and its dominant, though these eventually give way to more varied cadences and the triumphant A major conclusion.

Giovanni Maria Nanino (c. 1543-1607), whose biography is given in Volume 10, is a comparatively simple and extrovert composer who writes in a compact polyphonic style with early baroque tendencies. His work is uniformly pleasant and easy to sing, and workmanlike in execution. The harmonies are plain, and tonal rather than modal; the ornamental cadences are a little predictable, but at least provide the pleasure of recognition. His joyful *Gloria in excelsis* is the second part of a double motet beginning *Hodie nobis caelorum Rex*. It was not published in Nanino's lifetime but survives in at least two manuscripts, the most authoritative being that in the Cappella Sistina, codex 72. The motet exhibits all the features mentioned above, and has an overall ease of movement, progressing from duple to the inevitable triple time for "Gaudet exercitus angelorum" and back again to the effortless duple sweep as it moves to the ebullient conclusion.

It is strange to think that, in his lifetime, Nanino had parity of esteem with Palestrina, a judgement which is unthinkable now, but this is to judge him by the highest standards of musical art. For though Palestrina occasionally nods, his mastery is undeniable, as can be seen in the motet which concludes this volume. *O magnum mysterium* is a comparatively early work, appearing in Palestrina's impressive *Liber primus . . . mottettorum quae partim quinis, partim senis, partim septenis vocibus concinantur,* Rome, 1569 (complete set of copies in the Bayersiche Staatsbibliothek, Munich). Of all the wealth of Renaissance settings for this moving text (here combined somewhat strangely with "Natum vidimus"), Palestrina's ranks with those of Victoria and Byrd (Volumes 3 and 6) as being among the best. It combines spaciousness with warmth and mystery, especially in its unusual opening, with a succession of raised leading notes and the single detached invocation in the bass. The vocal combinations are constantly varied for each text repetition, as if providing a multifaceted vocal meditation, as in "et admirabile sacramentum". Palestrina moves effortlessly into the new section "Natum vidimus" without any change of pace, reserving his triple section for "collaudantes Dominum", at the end of which he provides the first *tutti* of the motet before moving into the delicate sequence of extended alleluias with the characteristic melismas on the final syllable (cf. Palestrina's *O beata,* Volume 10).

Table of use according to the Tridentine Rite

Motet	Liturgical source	Seasonal or festal use
Ad te levavi	Offertory, 1st Sunday of Advent	Advent
Rorate caeli	1st ant., lauds, last Wednes. Advent	Advent
Domine Dominus noster	psalm, prime, Advent	Advent, Sundays after Pent., general
Veni Domine	combined office antiphons, Advent	Advent
Pastores loquebantur	Gospel, 2nd mass of Christmas	Christmas
Verbum caro factum est	8th respon., matins of Christmas	Christmas, communion, general
Gloria in excelsis	2nd part of 1st respon., matins of Christmas	Christmas
O magnum mysterium	4th respon., matins of Christmas combined with part of 3rd respon., matins of Christmas	Christmas, Circumcision

INDEX TO BOOKS 1-16

Composer	Motet	Voices	Book	Page	Seasonal and Festal Use
Gregor Aichinger	FACTUS EST REPENTE	SATB	4	2	Pentecost; Votive Mass, Holy Spirit; Confirmation
	REGINA CAELI	SATB	4	7	Easter; Blessed Virgin
Blasius Amon	MAGI VIDENTES STELLAM	SSATB	11	23	Epiphany
Felice Anerio	CHRISTUS FACTUS EST	SATB	1	1	Lent; Passiontide; general
Giovanni Francesco Anerio	REQUIEM AETERNAM	SATB	1	4	All Souls; funerals
Jacob Arcadelt	HAEC DIES	SATB	5	2	Easter
Giovanni Matteo Asola	DEUS CANTICUM NOVUM	SSA	7	2	general
	O VOS OMNES	SSA	7	6	Holy Week; Lent
William Byrd	ASPICE DOMINE	SSAATB	13	2	Lent; Passiontide; funerals
	AVE VERUM	SATB	2	2	Corpus Christi; Communion; general
	BEATA VISCERA	SAATB	12	20	Christmas; Blessed Virgin
	CIBAVIT EOS	SATB	2	6	Corpus Cristi; Communion; general
	CONFIRMA HOC DEUS	SSATB	9	2	Pentecost; Votive Mass, Holy Spirit
	JUSTORUM ANIMAE	SSATB	9	5	All Saints; feasts of martyrs
	MEMENTO SALUS AUCTOR	SSA	7	8	Christmas; Blessed Virgin
	O LUX BEATA TRINITAS	SSAATB	13	11	Trinity; general
	O MAGNUM MYSTERIUM	SATB	6	2	Christmas; Circumcision
	SENEX PUERUM	SATB	2	10	Purification
	TERRA TREMÜIT	SSATB	9	8	Easter
	VENITE COMEDITE	SATB	2	13	Corpus Christi; Communion; general
Clemens non Papa	AVE MARIA	SSATB	11	2	Blessed Virgin; Advent; Annunciation
	CRUX FIDELIS	SATB	5	5	Lent and Passiontide; Feasts of the Cross
	MAGI VENIUNT	SATB	6	5	Epiphany
	EGO FLOS CAMPI	SSA	7	13	Blessed Virgin
Loyset Compère	VERBUM CARO FACTUM EST	SATB	6	9	Christmas; general
Jean Conseil (Consilium)	ADJUVA ME DOMINE	SATB	8	2	Lent; general
Francesco Corteccia	SURGE ILLUMINARE JERUSALEM	SSATB	12	23	Epiphany; Christmas
Alessandro Costantini	CONFITEMINI DOMINO	SSA	7	16	general
Couillart	VIRI GALILEI	SATB	8	5	Ascension
Giovanni Croce	O SACRUM CONVIVIUM	SATB	1	6	Corpus Christi; Communion, except in Lent
Richard Dering	AVE VIRGO GLORIOSA	SSATB	9	10	Blessed Virgin
	JUBILATE DEO	SSAATB	13	15	Christmas; Epiphany; general
François Dulot	MARIA MAGDALENE	SATB	8	8	Easter
Juan Esquivel	DUO SERAPHIM	SSAATB	14	27	Trinity; general
	EGO SUM PANIS VIVUS	SATB	3	2	Corpus Christi; Communion
	REPLETI SUNT OMNES	SSATB	10	25	Pentecost; Holy Spirit
	TRIA SUNT MUNERA	SSATB	12	27	Epiphany; Christmas
Costanzo Festa	DOMINATOR COELORUM	SSATB	10	2	time of war; general
Giovanni Gabrieli	EXAUDI DOMINE	SSAATB	14	2	penitential; general
Mathieu Gascogne	CARO MEA	SATB	8	12	Corpus Christi; Communion
Elzéar Genet (Carpentras)	RECORDARE DOMINE	SSA	7	19	Holy Week; Lent
	SEDERUNT IN TERRA	SSA	7	21	Holy Week; Lent
Claude Goudimel	GLORIA IN EXCELSIS	SATB	8	17	Christmas
Francisco Guerrero	CANITE TUBA	SATB	3	5	Advent
	GLORIOSE CONFESSOR	SATB	3	9	St. Dominic; Confessors
	PASTORES LOQUEBANTUR	SSATBB	16	21	Christmas
	RORATE CAELI	SATB	6	10	Advent
Andrzej Hakenberger	AD TE DOMINE LEVAVI	SSATBB	16	2	Advent
	EXSULTATE JUSTI	SSATBar.B	15	24	general

Composer	Motet	Voices	Book	Page	Seasonal and Festal Use
Jacob Handl	ECCE CONCIPIES	SATB	4	9	Advent
	ECCE QUOMODO	SATB	4	12	Passiontide; Lent
	IN NOMINE JESU	SAATB	11	28	Holy Name; Christ
	LAETENTUR CAELI	SSAATB	15	30	Christmas; general
	ORIETUR STELLA	SSATB	12	2	Advent
	RESONET IN LAUDIBUS	SATB	4	15	Christmas
	RORATE CAELI	SSATBB	16	7	Advent
Hans Leo Hassler	CANTATE DOMINO	SATB	4	18	Christmas; general
	CANTATE DOMINO	SSATB	11	32	Christmas; general
	DIXIT MARIA	SATB	6	14	Annunciation; Advent
	LAETENTUR CAELI	SATB	4	21	Christmas
	TU ES PETRUS	SATB	4	24	St. Peter and Paul; general
	VERBUM CARO FACTUM EST	SSAATB	16	27	Christmas; Communion; general
Marc' Antonio Ingegneri	IN MONTE OLIVETI	SATB	1	10	Lent; Passiontide
Heinrich Isaac	ECCE VIRGO CONCIPIES	SATB	6	18	Advent
	GUSTATE ET VIDETE	SATB	5	9	Communion; general
	JERUSALEM SURGE	SATB	5	11	Advent
Jachet of Mantua	O VOS OMNES	SATB	8	21	Holy Week; Lent
Robert Johnson	DUM TRANSISSET	SATB	2	16	Easter
Josquin des Près	AVE MARIA	SATB	5	13	Blessed Virgin; Advent; Annunciation
	TU SOLUS	SATB	5	21	Christ; Passiontide; general
Orlandus Lassus	ADORAMUS TE CHRISTE	SSA	7	24	Holy Week; Lent; general
	ALMA REDEMPTORIS	SSATB	12	6	Advent to Purification
	DOMINE DOMINUS NOSTER	SSAATB	16	11	Advent; Sundays after Pentecost; general
	IMPROPERIUM	SATB	5	25	Passiontide; Lent
	IN PACE	SSA	7	26	Evening service
	JUBILATE DEO	SATB	5	28	Christmas; Epiphany; general
	JUSTORUM ANIMAE	SSATB	11	6	All Saints; feasts of martyrs
	SCIO ENIM	SATB	5	31	funerals; Easter; general
Leonhard Lechner	NOVIT DOMINUS	SSAATB	15	33	general
Jean Lhéritier	SANCTA MARIA	SATB	8	23	Blessed Virgin
Antoine de Longueval	BENEDICITE DEUM CAELI	SATB	8	28	general rejoicing
Luca Marenzio	HODIE CHRISTUS NATUS EST	SATB	6	20	Christmas
	O REX GLORIAE	SATB	1	13	Ascension
	TRIBUS MIRACULIS	SATB	1	16	Epiphany to Septuagesima
Claudio Merulo	PECCANTEM ME QUOTIDIE	SSAATB	14	9	All souls; funerals; Lent
Philippe de Monte	FACTUM EST SILENTIUM	SSAATB	15	2	St. Michael; general
	PECCANTEM ME QUOTIDIE	SSATB	11	10	All Souls; funerals; Lent
Claudio Monteverdi	AVE MARIA	SSA	7	29	Blessed Virgin; Advent; Annunciation
	LAUDA SION	SSA	7	30	Blessed Sacrament
Cristóbal de Morales	DOMINE DEUS	SSA	7	33	Christ; general
	ECCE SIC BENEDICETUR	SSAATB	14	22	Nuptial Mass; general
	IN DIE TRIBULATIONIS	SSA	7	35	Lent; general
	MANUS TUAE DOMINE	SSATB	10	28	funerals; Lent
	PECCANTEM ME QUOTIDIE	SATB	3	13	All souls; funerals; Lent
	REGINA CAELI	SATB	3	16	Easter; Blessed Virgin
	SIMILE EST REGNUM	SATB	3	19	Septuagesima; general
	VENI DOMINE	SSAATB	16	17	Advent
Thomas Morley	AGNUS DEI	SATB	2	20	general
	LABORAVI IN GEMITU	SSAATB	13	21	Lent; general
Jean Mouton	REGES TERRAE	SATB	8	31	Epiphany; Christmas
William Mundy	ADOLESCENTULUS SUM EGO	SAATBB	13	29	general
Giovanni Maria Nanino	ADORAMUS TE CHRISTE	SSATB	10	6	Good Friday; Lent; general
	GLORIA IN EXCELSIS	SMez.Mez.ATB	16	32	Christmas
Diego Ortiz	JANITOR CAELI	SATB	3	23	St. Peter and Paul

Composer	Motet	Voices	Book	Page	Seasonal and Festal Use
G.P.da Palestrina	ALMA REDEMPTORIS	SATB	1	20	Advent to Purification
	CANITE TUBA	SSATB	12	10	Advent
	DIES SANCTIFICATUS	SATB	6	25	Christmas
	EGO SUM PANIS VIVUS	SATB	1	23	Corpus Christi; Communion
	JESU REX ADMIRABILIS	SSA	7	40	Christ; Christmas; Easter; Ascension
	O BEATA TRINITAS	SSATB	10	10	Trinity Sunday; general
	O MAGNUM MYSTERIUM	SSAATB	16	36	Christmas; Circumcision
	SICUT CERVUS	SATB	1	27	Holy Saturday; Communion; general
	SUPER FLUMINA	SATB	1	31	20th Sunday after Pentecost; Lent
	TUA JESU DILECTIO	SSA	7	41	Christ; Christmas; Easter; Ascension
	TU ES PETRUS	SSATBB	14	15	St. Peter and Paul; general
Pierre Passereau	AUXILIUM MEUM	SATB	— 8	35	Advent; general
Juan Ginés Perez	GLORIA LAUS	SSATB	10	34	Palm Sunday; Christ the King
Peter Philips	O BEATUM ET SACROSANCTUM DIEM	SSATB	12	30	Christmas
	TIBI LAUS	SSATB	9	14	Trinity Sunday; general
Costanzo Porta	EGO SUM PASTOR BONUS	SSAATB	14	22	Eastertide; Communion; general
	VOCE MEA	SSATB	10	17	Lent; general
Michael Praetorius	OMNIS MUNDUS JOCUNDETUR	SATB	6	30	Christmas
	PUER NATUS	SATB	4	28	Christmas
	SALVE REX NOSTER	SATB	4	29	general
Robert Ramsey	O SAPIENTIA	SSATB	12	16	Advent; Pentecost
Andreas Raselius	ERIPE ME DE INIMICIS	SSATB	11	38	Holy Week, All Souls; Lent
Thomas Ravenscroft	Four rounds from PAMMELIA	5 voices	13	41	various
Jacob Regnart	PROPE EST DOMINUS	SATB	6	32	Advent
	STETIT JESUS	SSATB	11	14	Easter
Adam Rener	VENI CREATOR SPIRITUS (QUI DICERIS PARACLITUS)	SSAT Bar.B	15	8	Pentecost; Holy Spirit; general
Martin de Rivafrecha	ANIMA MEA	SATB	3	26	Blessed Virgin
Philippe Rogier	RECORDATUS EST	SSAATB	15	12	Christmas; general
Cipriano de Rore	JUBILATE DEO	SAATB	11	19	Christmas; general
Ludwig Senfl	DEUS IN ADJUTORIUM	SATB	4	34	general
Claudin de Sermisy	BENEDIC ANIMA MEA	SATB	— 8	39	general rejoicing
John Shepherd	IN MANUS TUAS	SATB	2	22	Compline; general
Francesco Soriano	REGINA CAELI	SATB	1	35	Easter
Jan Sweelinck	HODIE CHRISTUS NATUS EST	SSATB	12	36	Christmas
Thomas Tallis	EUGE CAELI	SATB	2	25	Feasts of the Blessed Virgin
	O NATA LUX	SSATB	9	21	Transfiguration; Communion; feasts of Christ
	O SACRUM CONVIVIUM	SAATB	9	23	Corpus Christi; Communion
	SANCTE DEUS	SATB	2	27	feasts of Our Lord; Lent & Passiontide; funerals
John Taverner	ALLELUIA	SATB	2	33	Easter; general excluding Lent
	AUDIVI	SATB	2	35	All Saints; Advent
Christopher Tye	GLORIA LAUS	SATB	2	38	Palm Sunday; Passiontide; Christ the King
	OMNES GENTES PLAUDITE	SMez. ATB	9	28	Ascension; general
	Part 2: PSALLITE DEO	SMez. ATB	9	33	Ascension; general
Jacob Vaet	O QUAM GLORIOSUM	SATB	5	35	All Saints; general
Cornelius Verdonck	AVE GRATIA PLENA	SATB	6	36	Blessed Virgin; Advent; Annunciation
Ludovico da Viadana	EXSULTATE JUSTI	SATB	1	37	general

Composer	Motet	Voices	Book	Page	Seasonal and Festal Use
Tomás Luis de Victoria	AVE MARIA	SATB	3	29	Blessed Virgin; Advent; Annunciation
	GAUDE VIRGO MARIA	SSATB	10	38	Blessed Virgin
	NE TIMEAS MARIA	SATB	6	38	Advent; Annunciation
	O DOMINE JESU CHRISTE	SSAATB	14	38	feasts of Christ; Communion; general
	O MAGNUM MYSTERIUM	SATB	3	32	Christmas to Epiphany
	O VOS OMNES	SATB	3	36	Holy Week; Lent
	PUERI HEBRAEORUM	SATB	3	38	Palm Sunday
Pietro Vinci	MIRABILE MYSTERIUM	SSATB	10	21	Christmas; Corpus Christi; Communion
Johann Walter	NUNC DIMITTIS (LUMEN AD REVELATIONEM)	SSAATB	15 ✓	37	Compline; general
	VERBUM CARO	SATB	4	39	Christmas; general
Giaches de Wert	PECCAVI SUPER NUMERUM	SSAATB	15 ✓	17	Lent; penitential
Robert White	AD TE LEVAVI	SSAATB	13	34	Lent; general
	PRECAMUR SANCTE DOMINE (CHRISTE QUI LUX ES)	SSATB	9	38	Evening service; general
Adrian Willaert	O MAGNUM MYSTERIUM	SATB	5	38	Christmas; Epiphany